D1607880

AUDREY HEPBURN

A Life from Beginning to End

Copyright © 2021 by Hourly History.

Table of Contents

Introduction

Audrey Kathleen Ruston, later known as Audrey Hepburn, was born on May 4, 1929, in Brussels, Belgium. Her parents divorced when she was six years old, and she didn't see her father for many years. In 1940, when she and her mother Ella lived in Arnhem, the Netherlands, the city was invaded by Nazis. There was little food or luxuries of any kind. As World War II dragged on, Audrey reportedly defied the Nazis by transporting forged identity papers in her school bag. No one ever suspected this charming, shy young girl.

At a young age, Audrey studied ballet and aspired to be a dancer. She even danced for Nazi audiences during the Second World War. Eventually though, it became obvious that Audrey's real talent lay in acting, and while working as a model in 1948, she was discovered and won a few small roles in movies. Before long, she was called to the United States, where her first movie, *Roman Holiday,* was an instant hit. From then on, her career skyrocketed. It was as if she were incapable of making a mistake onscreen.

Audrey married fellow actor Mel Ferrer in 1954. While Ferrer struggled to advance his career, Audrey's movies *The Nun's Story*, *Charade*, *My Fair Lady*, and *Breakfast at Tiffany's* were all hits. Her inherent beauty and grace made her a natural for the screen. Audiences everywhere adored her.

Audrey and Ferrer divorced in 1968. The following year, she married an Italian doctor, Andrea Mario Dotti, with whom she had a son named Luca. She and Dotti eventually divorced in 1982. Now semi-retired from acting, Audrey became active as an ambassador in UNICEF and worked with starving and poverty-stricken children in Africa. During her illustrious film career, she made over thirty movies, was nominated for six Oscars, and won two.

Chapter One

Born into War

"I can testify to what UNICEF means to children because I was among those who received food and medical relief right after World War II."

—Audrey Hepburn

The world's most famous gamine was born in Brussels, Belgium, on May 4, 1929. Audrey Kathleen Ruston, later known as Audrey Hepburn, was born to a British-Austrian father and a Dutch mother, making her a British subject. Her father, Joseph Ruston, was an upper-class bourgeois who tried to make a success of himself in the diplomatic services and later as a banker in various European countries. Thanks to this, Audrey was fluent in several languages before the age of six.

Audrey's mother, Baroness Ella van Heemstra, a divorced mother of two sons, was related to the Dutch reigning royal family. Ella's reasons for marrying a commoner are not known, but Joseph Ruston could be quite charming, and besides, he (wrongly) believed himself to be related to James Hepburn, the third husband of Mary, Queen of Scots. It was Ella who insisted he incorporate the name Hepburn into the family name. Undoubtedly because of her social rank, she held the dominant position in the family.

The first half-dozen years of Audrey's life were spent in splendid mansions due to her royal connections. Although she sometimes traveled with her father, she was closer to her mother and was spoiled by her older half-brothers, who adored their little sister. Since the boys were her main companions, Audrey developed into a tree-climbing tomboy who cared nothing about dolls and fancy dresses. She also loved music and would play the piano for company. It was a loving and secure childhood which would soon be cut short.

In 1935, the tumultuous political situation in Europe would have been beyond the understanding of six-year-old Audrey. Mussolini was introducing fascism to Spain, and Hitler was making ominous noises in Germany.

As her parents increased their business travel, they spent more and more time in London. While staying in the city, both Joseph and Ella developed a fervent passion for Oswald Mosley, the leader of Britain's Fascist Party. It must be remembered that, at the time, fascism was not considered evil and was preferred over communism. Nevertheless, Mosley's "Blackshirts" were fashioned after Hitler's Brownshirts and caused frequent riots and skirmishes in London.

Both of Audrey's parents became members of the British Union of Fascists. Mosley came from a noble family, like Ella, which gave her immediate access to the top echelon and inner circle of British fascists. She wrote a magazine article about Oswald Mosley in which she stated, "And we who are following Sir Oswald Mosley know that in him we have found a leader whose eyes are not riveted on earthly things, whose inspiration is of a higher plane, and whose idealism will carry Britain into the bright light."

By the end of the year, Audrey's idyllic life would be shattered when her father abruptly left the family. He simply walked out one day, never to return. With this, Audrey's existence was turned upside down, and she later described it as "one of the great traumas of my life. It left a very deep scar on me."

The reason for Joseph's permanent exile from the home has never been fully explained, and Audrey herself never spoke of it. People who knew her parents indicated that Ella's father, Baron van Heemstra, was horrified at his daughter's public involvement with fascist ideology and blamed Joseph. Since Joseph managed Ella's wealth (as most husbands did at the time), the Baron could easily have threatened embezzlement or financial malfeasance to force Joseph to leave.

In any case, the protracted divorce took several years, making its way through both Dutch and British courts. Joseph wanted Audrey to continue her education in Britain, so while her mother moved back to the Netherlands, Audrey traveled to Kent to study at a small private school in Elham. This was especially painful for Audrey, who was very close to her mother. As she started school in Britain, she turned from a carefree child into a shy loner.

When Ella visited Britain and saw Audrey for the first time in six months, she was shocked at the change in her little girl. She became so concerned that she moved to a boardinghouse in Elham to be close to her daughter. The girl immediately began to blossom again in the company of her mother.

Joseph and Ella's divorce was finalized in 1938, just as the war in Europe was threatening to erupt. Ella was worried about Audrey's safety, and since the Netherlands was a neutral country, Ella had her father make arrangements to fly both of them out of Britain without Joseph's permission. They found a home in the town of Arnhem. For a short time, Audrey was safe, but it would be many decades until she saw her father again. Clearly, her perfect childhood was coming to an abrupt end.

The transition was difficult for Audrey, who didn't speak much Dutch. She had to catch up quickly. When she did, school became much more enjoyable. She also enjoyed the ballet classes in which her mother enrolled her. However, as it turned out, Audrey would have been safer remaining in Britain, a country that the Nazis were never able to conquer. The Netherlands, on the other hand, was a valuable trading post and had resources that the Germans coveted.

Early in 1940, the Nazis had conquered Denmark. Neutral Holland no longer seemed to be such a safe haven. On May 10, Audrey awoke to the roar of airplanes soaring past overhead. Her mother tried to convince her that they were German planes on their way to Britain. The aircraft were indeed German, but they were not flying quite that far. They were launching an attack on the Netherlands' most important seaport, Rotterdam. Thousands of people died, and many thousands more were wounded.

The Dutch army and naval forces fought fiercely against the invaders, while the official government set up a government-in-exile in London. Germany seized The Hague four days later. Radios were forbidden, and citizens had no news except permitted German propaganda. Soon enough, armored cars with machine guns rolled through the once peaceful town of Arnhem. The Baron, Audrey's grandfather, had to open his mansion to German soldiers.

Audrey felt the direct consequences of the new regime at school. Jewish teachers were disappearing, and the curriculum now had a decided Nazi bias. She continued her ballet classes, and dancing seemed to be her only future. As a British citizen, Audrey was an enemy of the Reich and qualified for internment. Ella warned her never to speak English and to start using the name Edda van Heemstra rather than her English-sounding name Audrey.

Back in Britain, Audrey's father Joseph had his own problems. As a leading fascist, he was rounded up by the British government and sent to jail. Subsequently, he was sent to a camp on the Isle of Man.

Seeing Nazism up close, Ella slowly reversed her former fascist enthusiasm. She tried to work with the resistance, but her reputation and previous adoration for Mosley preceded her. She was never fully trusted.

Audrey, innocent and doe-eyed, was another story. At 15, she now performed at a number of dance recitals. This afforded her more freedom of movement than most people had, and she soon began to deliver forged identity papers wherever directed. She hid the documents in her bookbag as no one was concerned with what a young girl was carrying. Already, she was using the charm for which she would later become famous. Occasionally, when she saw Nazi guards, she would pick some flowers and handed them a bouquet with the sweetest of smiles— a strange beginning to her future acting career.

In 1942, as living in Arnhem became increasingly perilous, Ella and Audrey escaped on foot by walking five miles to the Baron's home in Velp. Food was rationed, soap was non-existent, and everyone went hungry and dirty. Audrey and Ella didn't eat proper meals again until the Allies liberated the Netherlands in 1945 and filled the churches with food and supplies.

Other members of the family were not as fortunate; Audrey's half-brother Ian had been sent to a German labor camp in Berlin, and her uncle Otto was executed for his suspected involvement in the resistance movement.

Chapter Two

Post-War Years

"I'm half-Irish, half-Dutch, and I was born in Belgium. If I was a dog, I'd be in a hell of a mess!"

—Audrey Hepburn

The war had left Audrey malnourished and perennially hungry. She began to gobble down anything edible, such as a whole jar of jam. When she volunteered at the local hospital where American soldiers were recovering, they handed her chocolate. One day, she ate seven candy bars in ten minutes and became sick.

The family slowly reassembled. Her older half-brother Alexander came out of hiding. The other brother, Ian, walked 350 miles from his internment camp in Berlin to reach home.

There was no word from her father. Ella couldn't care less about her ex-husband, but Audrey was determined to find him. She wouldn't succeed until many decades later when she sought help from the Red Cross and discovered that Joseph was alive and living in Ireland. He had made no effort to contact his daughter, which left Audrey feeling rejected.

Survival after the war wasn't much easier than surviving the bombing and occupation. The Baron's finances were tied up by the Nazis, so he could no longer help. Ella hoped for opportunities in the capital, Amsterdam, but thousands of others had the same idea. The once-proud Baroness considered herself lucky to find a job as a live-in housekeeper. She soon left her job as a housekeeper though—she'd never taken orders in her life and was incapable of doing so. She eventually became the manager of a florist shop.

Audrey, still unseemly thin, progressed with her dancing and performed in an afternoon show at the Hortus Theater in 1946. She didn't startle the world of dance, but critics did find her pleasing.

In 1947, two years after the end of the war, life was still a struggle. Ella now worked in a beauty salon. Audrey began designing and making hats for her mother's customers as a means of earning more money. She was marvelously creative and sold quite a few hats.

By accident, she learned that she might qualify for a scholarship in London with the famed ballerina, Marie Rambert, who had taught

Fontaine and Nijinsky. While going through the necessary red tape and paperwork, Audrey landed a role as a guide in 30-minute travelogues. It wasn't anything major, and all that the studio requested was a pretty girl. Nevertheless, Audrey's bright personality was a perfect fit. She also worked as a model, although she still hoped for a career in ballet.

Papers for Ella and Audrey to go to Britain were difficult to get, as the British had not forgotten Ella's pro-fascist ideology. Finally, in December of 1948, mother and daughter sailed across the waters from The Hague to London. Once they arrived, they did not waste time. The two, who had spent their lives in luxurious surroundings, headed straight to a cheap bed and breakfast. Then, they went to see Marie Rambert.

Rambert gave them a tour of the school while Ella and Audrey shared their war experiences. Afterward, Audrey did an audition. Rambert didn't comment on Audrey's talent, or lack of it. She was impressed enough with the girl's radiant looks and natural grace to offer a partial scholarship.

Nevertheless, life in post-war London was harsh. Food rations were barely enough to sustain life, and the city was damp and foggy. In addition, Ella, who was not a citizen, could not get a work permit. She eventually persuaded an old acquaintance to let her manage an apartment building off the books. Audrey meanwhile worked part-time as a receptionist.

Although she enjoyed her dance lessons, it was clear that Audrey was growing too tall to become a prima ballerina. Instead, the classes brought her into contact with other students who were pursuing careers in stage and film. One day, Audrey took the underground to the Hippodrome Theatre, where hundreds of others were waiting to be cast in the musical

High Button Shoes. Fortunately, Audrey's talents were impressive enough to get her hired as a chorus girl. It wasn't ballet, but for the first time, Audrey was earning money as a performer. Her life, so hard and joyless during the war years, was looking up.

The actor Cecil Landeau had a front-row seat to one of her performances. To him, Audrey stood out from the rest of the chorus. He obtained her name in the event he could use her in his next production.

Chapter Three

Early Work

"As a child, I was taught that it was bad manners to bring attention to yourself, and to never, ever make a spectacle of yourself . . . All of which I've earned a living doing.

—Audrey Hepburn

Audrey's chance came in the spring of 1949 when Cecil Landeau hired her for a role in the chorus of his play, *Sauce Tartare,* where her long legs were on display during all the dance numbers. Somehow, she received all the attention. Clearly, the inexperienced Audrey was taking London by storm.

Finding herself in a hit assured that she would receive other offers. Conversely, Audrey's success on stage increased her demand as a model, and in 1950, she ended up appearing in British *Vogue*. It was time to think seriously about her future.

Cecil Landeau took notice of Audrey's popularity and considered her for a larger part in his next play, *Sauce Piquante*. Audrey found the idea amusing. She had little experience, and her upbringing had left her with a noticeable accent. Not to be deterred,

Landeau paid for acting and speech lessons.

The other actresses in *Sauce Piquante* complained that although they were far more amply endowed, the audience was constantly looking at Audrey, who looked radiant and divine. One girl lamented, "We don't stand a chance when she's on stage. We might just as well stay in our dressing room." Although she was one of the lesser dancers in the show, all eyes were invariably on Audrey Hepburn.

Audrey was by now 21 and, thus far, had experienced no romance in her life. That was about to change. Singer Marcel LeBon began leaving a rose in her dressing room before every performance. Audrey was soon smitten, and the two began a relationship. There were even rumors of marriage.

Audrey's great supporter, Landeau, however, threatened to sue if she married. He ridiculously claimed that the audience who came to see the scantily clad women wanted them to be single. Landeau was either jealous or wanted the extra publicity for his show. Since all the gossip columns carried the story, he certainly received enough publicity. In the end though, it didn't matter because the romance fizzled out all on its own.

Soon after, Audrey met James Hanson, the scion of one of Britain's most prominent families and one of Europe's most eligible bachelors. Everyone was in favor of this match. No fool, Audrey understood that if she were to marry into such as illustrious family, she would have to give up any acting aspirations. For the time being, she didn't have to make any decisions and simply enjoyed the romance.

In 1951, Audrey had a small role opposite Alex Guinness in *The Lavender Hill Mob.* Like so many men,

Alex was smitten by Audrey and introduced her to MGM's casting director, Melvyn LeRoy, who was in London. LeRoy was, however, unimpressed and didn't take the meeting any further. Undeterred, Audrey continued acting in British and French movies.

One evening, she was approached by French writer Colette, who was working with Anita Loos on the Broadway production of the play *Gigi*. The story of *Gigi* is a tad risqué. Gigi is a 16-year-old schoolgirl being guided and coached by a group of experienced courtesans to become a mistress and learn all the necessary etiquette involved in pleasing a man. For the storyline to work, Gigi has to look like an innocent child.

For her part, Gigi enjoys spending time with a frivolous young man named Gaston and has no interest in becoming some old man's darling. She prefers the company of Gaston, but he doesn't rate as marriage material. In the end, Gaston is so charmed by Gigi that he ends up offering her a reputable marriage.

At the same time as negotiations began for Audrey to go to America and star as the lead in *Gigi*, her first Broadway show, director William

Wyler was in Europe scouting out the lead for his next movie, *Roman Holiday.* Wyler immediately loved Audrey for the role. The role called for vulnerability, something which Audrey acted with ease, and she got to show her comic side as well when auditioning for the role of Princess Ann.

At the age of 22, Audrey had only played minor parts. She'd never set foot in America. Now, she was on her way across the ocean to tackle two iconic leading roles—*Gigi* for the stage and *Roman Holiday* for the screen. It was impossible to resist Audrey Hepburn. It wouldn't be long before she'd charm an entirely new continent.

Chapter Four

Debuting in Broadway and Hollywood

"I am proud to have been in a business that gives pleasure, creates beauty, and awakens our conscience, arouses compassion, and perhaps most importantly, gives millions a respite from our so violent world."

—Audrey Hepburn

After Audrey finished up packing for her tour in America, she crossed the Atlantic in the *Queen Mary* and landed in New York, staying at the Blackstone Hotel. She and James Hanson were still very much in love, and it was assumed she would return to Europe once her obligations in America had been met. There was no need to look for an apartment, she thought.

Gigi was scheduled to open at the Fulton Theater in November. Writer Anita Loos was so anxious for her play to become successful that she asked her friend, legendary screen director George Cukor, to come to New York and direct Audrey's performance. Unfortunately, he was unable to do so. Audrey, now acting in a foreign country in what was essentially a foreign language, would need plenty of coaching.

Ultimately, Raymond Rouleau, a French director, was called. It was thought that since both Rouleau and Audrey spoke French, this would make matters easier for her. Unfortunately, much of the rehearsal turned into bilingual confusion. Audrey now would have to learn the play in two separate languages. Eventually, the great Cathleen Nesbitt, who was playing one of the courtesan aunts, would take Audrey under her wings and coach her in her own apartment.

Audrey's inexperience became obvious as soon as Rouleau took over as director. She had no idea how to project her lines, fumbled her entrances, and essentially didn't understand much of the dialogue. Acting on Broadway was totally different than the minor screen roles she had previously done. She had no idea how to handle herself. At one point, she was even dismissed, but since it was too late to find a suitable replacement, she was called back.

Rouleau attempted to salvage the play. He played up Audrey's innocence and charm and turned the staging into a kind of ballet. Although Audrey's acting wasn't quite on par, it helped that she looked like Gigi. When *Gigi* opened at the Fulton Theater following out-of-town tryouts, it received rave reviews. Audrey's mother Ella and boyfriend Hanson were at the premiere, but Audrey did not need her own cheering section; she'd become a star on the first try. The following night, Audrey had her name in lights above the title. When she saw her name light up the marquee, she sighed. "Oh dear, and I still have to learn how to act."

If the show was going to be a hit—and it seemed to be heading in that direction—Audrey knew she and her boyfriend Hanson would be separated for a while. She was willing to accept that. One night over dinner, Hanson proposed marriage, and she accepted.

On the West Coast, Paramount Pictures watched Audrey's development with interest. They had her under contract for *Roman Holiday,* but they were now wondering if they shouldn't offer this fascinating newcomer a seven-year contract.

Although Audrey hated interviews, she was now a minor celebrity, and talking to the press was to become a part of her life. During one lunch interview, she discussed her experience with wartime deprivation while devouring corned beef hash, several eggs, several rolls, and a large dish of coffee ice cream. Audrey was clearly determined not to go hungry again.

Gigi closed after 219 performances, and Audrey prepared to go to Italy, where *Roman Holiday* would be filmed. Prior to her departure, Paramount flew in their chief clothing designer, Edith Head, to arrange for customs for her movie.

Roman Holiday is a romantic comedy set in Italy. Audrey plays a princess, Ann, who is frustrated with royal protocol. She sneaks out of the palace to experience some real-life fun in

Rome. This is after her chaperone has given her a sleeping pill.

Gregory Peck plays a reporter named Joe in desperate need of a story. When an inadvertently dizzy and drugged Audrey ends up in his apartment, he learns who she is and sees the story of a lifetime. The pictures he takes of her in a state of dishabille will thrill his editor. The following day, they see the sights of Rome. They get to know each other and eventually fall in love. Everything that happens during their interlude is photographed by Joe and his photographer friend—and not in a flattering way for a proper princess.

Their time together ends when Ann is located by embassy staff.

The princess returns to the embassy and has a press conference trying to explain her absence the prior day. She remembers more about her unseemly behavior and is afraid it will come to light. During the press conference, Joe, who is among the horde of reporters, steps forward and hands her an envelope, which contains all the incriminating photos of Ann. He has decided that ruining Ann's reputation in exchange for some sensational news story is not worth it. Besides, he truly does love her. Ann is grateful and wistfully watches him turn and walk away. She knows they will never meet again.

Gregory Peck was the known star, and Audrey Hepburn the unknown newcomer. However, it was Peck who insisted that Audrey's name be placed with his above the title. He did not doubt that her fame would skyrocket. It was a very generous act.

Following the filming in Rome, Audrey had to rush back to America for the road tour of *Gigi*. Hanson visited her at Christmastime in Chicago. The details are unknown, but when he returned to London, there was an announcement that their engagement was officially off.

After the tour, Audrey went to Hollywood. Paramount offered her a seven-year contract, script approval on all movies, and time off to do more theater. Few newcomers were granted such amenities, but everyone simply adored Audrey. She could do no wrong.

Audrey was committed to living in America, but Britain was still officially her home. When she returned there to visit her mother, Gregory Peck was coincidentally shooting in London. The Pecks threw Audrey a welcome-home party and introduced her to the actor Mel Ferrer. Audrey and Ferrer had much in common and spent a great deal of time talking. Ferrer had a wife and children back in the U.S., but the two were instantly attracted to each other.

Chapter Five

Rise to Super Stardom

"I believe, every day, you should have at least one exquisite moment."

—Audrey Hepburn

The premiere of *Roman Holiday* at the Radio City Music Hall was another winner for Audrey. Paramount insisted she do an interview and cover story with *Time* magazine, an unusual request when such interviews were normally done by established actresses such as Elizabeth Taylor. Readers couldn't get enough of Audrey's fragile beauty.

She soon began filming her second American movie, *Sabrina*, the story of a chauffeur's daughter being pursued by the family's two sons, played by Humphrey Bogart and William Holden. Although the story is about this romantic triangle, another star of the movie is the wardrobe created especially by emerging designer Hubert de Givenchy. Givenchy and Audrey's relationship would last for many years as he designed the perfect outfits to highlight her figure.

In the film, Sabrina has been in love with playboy David, played by Holden, for years, although he has never paid any attention to her. She goes ahead with her plans to sail to Paris and study at the Cordon Bleu. When she returns, she has changed into a young sophisticate dressed in Givenchy designs. David, who doesn't even recognize her and is engaged, immediately begins to flirt with her.

His older brother, Linus, played by Bogart, is a serious businessman. He tries to prevent an affair between them because David's engagement holds tremendous potential for their business. The fact is, Linus has fallen for Sabrina but refuses to admit it to himself. In the end, Sabrina decides to leave permanently and return to Paris. David, who realizes his brother is truly in love and not just flirting, arranges for Linus and Sabrina to sail to Paris together.

The atmosphere off-screen was totally different than the one on-screen. Bogart was in a particularly foul mood throughout the shooting and frequently drunk—nothing at all like his gruff but charming character on-screen. Audrey didn't develop even a casual relationship with him. It was William Holden who caught Audrey's attention. He was, however, married and eager to maintain the image of a good family man.

Nevertheless, Audrey fell hard for Holden and was captivated by his charm. As they began an affair, she had serious daydreams about him, including dreams of the two of them getting married. Although Holden admired Audrey, including the fact that she was 11 years younger than he was, he had no intentions of getting a divorce. He even brought her home to meet his wife, Ardis, who knew what was happening.

Meanwhile, the now-divorced Mel Ferrer was lurking patiently in the background. He sent Audrey a copy of the play *Ondine* and suggested that the two of them might be perfect for the lead. The play had been a success in Paris before the war. Audrey loved the storyline. It's a medieval fairy tale of a knight, Hans, who falls for a water nymph, Ondine, and marries her. He is unaware that Ondine has been cursed and that any man who isn't true to her will die. When the knight becomes involved with another woman, he dies while she continues to live in her underwater kingdom.

The part of the water nymph was perfect for Audrey, and she knew it immediately. Wisely, Audrey had insisted in her contract with Paramount that she be permitted to do an annual play, so she was able to do *Ondine*. They met for rehearsals in New York. Audrey was still hurting from her affair with Holden, and seeing Mel Ferrer again, to whom she'd previously been attracted, helped heal the wounds. They soon began a relationship.

They were direct opposites in character. Mel was macho and experienced, while Audrey was fragile and still learning. He was domineering; she was shy. He took the lead in the relationship and guided her professionally. During rehearsal, he even began to direct Audrey's performance instead of letting the director, Alfred Lunt, do the job. This created friction between the men but probably helped Audrey. This was, after all, only her second Broadway play.

Ondine premiered on February 18, 1954, and became an immediate hit. Audrey especially stood out. According to the *New York Times*, "Miss Hepburn is able to translate [its intangibles] into the language of the theatre without artfulness or precociousness. She gives a pulsing performance that is all grace and enchantment, disciplined by an instinct for the realities of the stage." It was Audrey who received cheers and curtain calls every night. Mel invariably joined her on stage for those calls. There were rumors that Mel was intimidated by Audrey's success and insisted on equal treatment.

While basking in the success of *Ondine,* Audrey learned that she had been nominated for an Academy Award for Best Actress thanks to her role in *Roman Holiday.* At the time, the Oscars were broadcast in New York at the Century Theatre. Sitting next to her mother, a delighted Audrey heard her name being called out as Best Actress.

Three days after winning the Oscar, Audrey won a Tony Award for her performance in *Ondine*. It must have seemed strange that only a decade earlier, Ella and Audrey were starving in war-ravaged Europe. Now, Audrey was winning prestigious awards for her second play and first major movie. Following the Tony Award, the producers insisted that the curtain calls would be by Audrey alone instead of with Mel. Mel was not happy.

Still, Audrey and Mel were a devoted couple. Friends, however, sensed Mel exerting control over Audrey's life. In the throes of love, nothing that Mel did upset Audrey. At the tender age of 25, she was still remarkably inexperienced in romance.

In June of 1954, Audrey's fragile health made it difficult for her to do nightly performances, and the play had to close. Audrey went to Switzerland to recover while Mel flew directly to Rome. After she sent him an expensive watch for his birthday, he flew to see her and asked her to marry him. Happily, she accepted. They made plans to marry as soon as Mel wrapped up his movie in Rome.

They were married in Burgenstock, Switzerland, on September 25, 1954.

Packs of reporters followed them to Rome and created disturbances until the couple posed for pictures. Following their honeymoon, they returned to Hollywood for the premiere of *Sabrina*. The movie was another hit for Audrey. During the less than five years that she'd spent in America, it was as if she couldn't do anything wrong.

When she became pregnant, Audrey was forced to put everything on hold due to her delicate health. Since Mel was doing a movie in London, they returned to Britain and moved into a six-room flat. Mel's problem was that his wife's short and limited career was outshining his. The publicist in London couldn't get him any publicity if it didn't include Audrey.

Chapter Six

Losing Her Child

"My own life has been much more than a fairy tale. I've had my share of difficult moments, but whatever difficulties I've gone through, I've always gotten the prize at the end."

—Audrey Hepburn

Audrey was trying to stay rested and enjoy a healthy pregnancy, but she couldn't escape the news that two different factions were planning to make an epic film based on Leo Tolstoy's *War and Peace*. Mike Todd was one director, and the other was the team of Carlo Ponti and Dino De Laurentiis. Both wanted Audrey for the role of Natasha Rostova in their separate movie. She hadn't signed with either team yet when Ponti and De Laurentiis offered the role of Prince Andrei to Mel if she would go with them. It was a sneaky move but effective.

Audrey immediately agreed to sign with Ponti and De Laurentiis if Paramount would lend her out. Paramount took it a step further and became a partner in the movie by adding to the financing. Paramount also threw in King Vidor to direct Audrey.

Nothing could begin until Audrey had her baby, but no one was in any hurry. There would be a lot of work to be done before they started filming anyway. Tolstoy's monster epic had to be reduced to under four hours. While Audrey waited, she received her second Oscar nomination for *Sabrina*. This time, she lost out to Grace Kelly. At around the same time, she miscarried. The reason is not known, but Audrey was devastated. It was a trauma she never discussed publicly.

By this point, De Laurentiis was already shooting the battle scenes for *War and Peace*. Mel and Audrey were reading and rereading Tolstoy's book to gain a better understanding of their characters. But turning Tolstoy's massive tome into a screenplay meant sacrificing much of the depth of character that is in the novel. During the film, Audrey is required to age from teenager to widow, which the still inexperienced actress managed admirably. She and Mel returned to Paris after the shooting was completed.

While in Paris, Audrey learned that Paramount wanted to lend her out to MGM for a collaboration with Fred Astaire in a movie called *Funny Face*. As a young girl, she had seen Astaire, one of the greatest song and dance men in history, in *Top Hat* and had enjoyed watching him. Now, Audrey would star opposite him as an equal. She plays a shy clerk named Jo Stockton working in a used bookstore in Greenwich Village. Astaire, who plays a photographer, wanders into the shop and decides to turn her into a model for one of his magazine shoots. As a model, Audrey gets to wear all kinds of incredible clothes. Once again, her friend Givenchy was there to dress her perfectly.

Although she was trained in ballet, Audrey was nervous to dance with someone like Astaire, who was one of the most famous dancers in

Hollywood. Fortunately, Astaire turned out to be very patient and helped her perfect her moves.

The release of *War and Peace*, however, proved to be difficult. The movie was three and a half hours long, and it was competing for viewing time with *80 Days Around the World*, Paramount's *The Ten Commandments,* and *Giant.* The fact was, theatergoers wanted to see Rock Hudson and Elizabeth Taylor in *Giant* rather than some long story by Tolstoy. To make matters worse, there appeared to be no spark between Audrey and Mel in the movie. Those who pictured the pair as the next Lunt and Fontanne developed severe doubts.

The couple refused to be deterred and went to California to make another movie together, *Mayerling*. Unfortunately, the director commented, "I had a lot of trouble getting them to turn on the heat. Audrey seemed to have a better rapport with that Yorkshire terrier of hers." Audrey did get praised for her performance, while Mel was widely panned.

Audrey took some time off to decide on her next venture. She accompanied Mel to Spain for his role in *The Sun Also Rises.* She enjoyed shopping and being simply a wife during the day while her husband was working.

Funny Face was released during this time while she was away from Hollywood with Mel. Even though the movie received only mediocre reviews (viewers objected to the pairing of the middle-aged Astaire and the mid-twenties Audrey), her Givenchy wardrobe did establish her reputation as one of the best-dressed women of the time.

After *The Sun Also Rises*, Mel went to Germany to film *Fraulein* with Dana

Wynter. Audrey remained in Los Angeles to study up on missionaries for her next movie, *The Nun's Story.*

Chapter Seven

Breakfast at Tiffany's

"I don't take my life seriously, but I do take what I do in my life seriously."

—Audrey Hepburn

The Nun's Story is based on the true story of Marie Louise Habets, a Belgian nun who left her religious order to join the resistance movement during World War II. Audrey was anxious to do this movie and met frequently with Habets to learn the necessary conducts and prayers that made up the daily existence of a nun. She lobbied for Mel in the role of the doctor, but the part went to Peter Finch.

Audrey plays Sister Luke, a woman from a well-to-do family who gives up everything to become a nun. She achieves her ambition to be sent to the Belgian Congo as a medical missionary. This turns into a disappointment when she realizes she will be working with the well-to-do white Europeans instead of the natives. There is an implied attraction between her and the doctor, which shocked many viewers. Sister Luke becomes greatly disappointed and disillusioned, but she is a hard worker and does her job.

As World War II breaks out, her vows demand that she not take any side in the matter. However, when her father dies at the hands of the Nazis, she can no longer obey her religious edicts. She leaves her order and becomes a regular woman again. Her future is unclear, but she is sure she is making the right decision.

Audrey immersed herself in the role, even spending some time in Marie Louise Habets' old convent. She lived without mirrors, radio, and television since such frivolities were not permitted by the order. She also visited the Belgian Congo to do some genuine background filming. Because of her fragile health, the visit terrified her. Audrey was a heavy smoker, even in her nun's costume. Frequently, she and the other nun actresses would gather for a cigarette break. A native, who took them for genuine nuns, became upset and complained. A production assistant told him that they were Americans as if that might explain away any strange behavior. The native nodded knowingly and continued on his way.

After six months of filming dressed in a nun's habit, Audrey was able to join Mel in Los Angeles and wear normal clothes again. She sincerely hoped that their time together would result in a successful pregnancy. Meanwhile, the couple attempted another movie collaboration. Mel directed Audrey in the movie *Green Mansions*, in which Audrey portrays a young jungle woman who falls in love with an escapee from Venezuelan rebels played by Anthony Perkins. She saves him from a snake bite on his leg. Her grandfather warns her he will leave after he heals. However, the two end up in love.

Following *Green Mansions*, Audrey and Mel spent some time in Los Angeles. Audrey wanted some rest, but she wouldn't get as much as she'd hoped for. United Artists offered her

$250,000 to co-star in the movie *The Unforgiven,* which was being directed by the legendary John Huston. She was unable to resist, although she was pregnant at the time.

Young Rachel Zachary, played by Audrey, is the daughter of white settlers. When someone spreads the rumor that Audrey is actual an Indian stolen from the Kiowa tribe at birth, the situation escalates into a war between the settlers and the Native Americans. When the truth comes out that she is indeed an Indian, many of the white settlers scorn her. The movie is not only an interesting western but unusual for the early

1960s as John Huston attempts to underscore the long-time prejudice against Native Americans.

While Audrey did manage to complete the movie, it turned into a personal tragedy when she fell off a horse. All production was stopped, and she was flown to Los Angeles on a stretcher. Still, she miscarried for a second time. Following *The Unforgiven,* Audrey took a year off in Switzerland to recover emotionally. She was too angry and too depressed for anything else. It was difficult for her to understand why she couldn't have children when she wanted them so much. Then, miraculously, she became pregnant again. At the same time, she gained her third Oscar nomination for *The Nun's Story*.

As Audrey was resting, Paramount kept sending her new scripts and reminding her that she owed them more movies. The manuscript that caught her attention was Truman Capote's *Breakfast at Tiffany's*. She wanted the role of Holly Golightly, a free spirit who dreams of a future with a millionaire.

The movie would, however, have to wait until after Audrey gave birth, which she did on July 17, 1960, when Sean Ferrer came into this world.

Audrey's hospital room was filled with congratulatory flowers from across the world. Audrey was beyond happy to finally have her wish fulfilled.

While Audrey was loving every moment of motherhood, preparations were underway for *Breakfast at Tiffany's*, the movie for which she became best known. Givenchy was hired to design her glamorous wardrobe, including the "little black dress" that the movie made famous. The new mother decided it was best for baby Sean to remain in Switzerland with his nanny and grandmother Ella while she and Mel went to film on location in New York City and then Hollywood.

Audrey was naturally an introvert, but she played the role of good-time party girl Holly exquisitely. Both Holly and her neighbor, played by George Peppard, yearn to be rich, hopefully by marrying someone with money. In the end, they are able to put their questionable past behind them and get together to build a genuine life.

By now, Audrey had unquestionably established herself as a bankable Hollywood star. When she made *The Children's Hour* in 1961, she was complimented on handling the topic of a pair of teachers accused of lesbianism with considerable sensitivity.

Following *The Children's Hour*, she made *Paris When It Sizzles* with her former co-star and lover William Holden. Both were married, and Audrey had no interest in any more dalliances. Not so Holden, who had deteriorated deeply into alcoholism. They were seen dining alone. Meanwhile, in Spain, Mel was enjoying the frequent company of a Duchess Quintanilla. There were rumors of infidelity on both sides.

Chapter Eight

Charade and My Fair Lady

"I may not always be offered work, but I'll always have my family."

—Audrey Hepburn

Directors and screenwriters had attempted to pair up Audrey and Cary Grant for a project three times previously. Each time, Grant turned it down, citing being uncomfortable with their age difference. He was 53 years old when he was finally persuaded to sign up for Stanley Donen's *Charade* because the writers adjusted the story to have Audrey chase after him instead of him pursuing her. Throughout the film, he keeps telling her he's too old.

Cary and Audrey's first meeting, in a restaurant, didn't go too well when she spilled a bottle of red wine over him. She spent the evening apologizing. Cary, ever the gentleman, sent a container of caviar the following day as an apology for making her feel bad.

By now, Audrey was reaching the top of the Hollywood ladder. She not only received $750,000 for making *Charade*, but she was able to negotiate a percentage of the gross earnings. In *Charade*, Audrey plays a woman who finds out her husband has been killed. It turns out several people are after some money he is supposed to have, and Audrey feels herself in danger. No one is who he appears to be, and everyone has a secret—even Cary Grant's character. He seems to pop in and out of her daily routine without a logical reason with several different identities. She has no idea who he is, but smitten, she keeps running after him while he unsuccessfully attempts to escape her clutches. Cary of the many names turns out to be in pursuit of the men who are after the money.

The press tried hard to create a romance between the two stars. However, Cary had just become involved with actress Dyan Cannon, who was playing on Broadway at the time, and was not after any other romantic entanglements. As a matter of fact, the Ferrers invited Cary and Dyan for an elegant New Year's Eve dinner in Paris after the shooting of *Charade*. Due to the popularity of both of its stars, *Charade* became an instant success and Audrey's biggest hit to date.

Both Mel and Audrey had been busy making movies and had spent very little time together or with their son,

Sean. The family hadn't seen much of each other, and Mel and Audrey needed to reestablish their relationship, which they did in their home in Switzerland in February. Sean, now three years old, had spent most of his life in Switzerland and was turning into a multilingual little charmer.

Their idyll ended when Audrey received the news that she was being offered the most sought-after female role since Scarlet O'Hara. Negotiations had been in place for months to put together the movie *My Fair Lady*. Audrey had hoped for the role of Eliza Doolittle, which had been made famous by Julie Andrews on Broadway, but her singing abilities were limited. It never occurred to her she might get the part. Still, Jack Warner insisted that no one but Audrey Hepburn would do. He had bought the screen rights to the movie for over $5 million, and while Julie Andrew had been a Broadway success, she was still relatively unknown; he wasn't willing to risk his investment on Julie. Audrey, on the other hand, was esteemed worldwide and a proven audience favorite.

Warner had to pay dearly for his star. Audrey's agent negotiated a million-dollar deal and a percentage of the gross. Rex Harrison, who had played the role of Professor Higgins opposite Julie Andrews, was rehired for the screen version. George Cukor was called on board to direct.

Since the shooting would take up to seven months, the Ferrer family rented a house in Los Angeles. To give Mel something to do, Audrey asked Warner to place him in some movie. Mel ended up with a feature role in *Sex and the Single Girl* for a mere $30,000. Professionally and personally, husband and wife seemed to be moving further apart.

For *My Fair Lady*, Cecil Beaton was in charge of Audrey's wardrobe. His designs were fantastic, but Audrey still showed them to Givenchy for final approval. Meanwhile, Cukor did his best with Audrey's limited singing ability. He had her mouth the words during filming and had her do the actual songs in the recording studio. Afterward, Warner covertly ordered that someone else be brought in to dub the songs. The professionally trained singer Marni Nixon was eventually used. Audrey was unhappy when she learned what Warner had done, but there was nothing for her to do but accept the reality that her singing simply wasn't what it needed to be for a first-rate musical.

The filming dragged on. Mel had finished his movie by now and resented having nothing to do, Sean had caught a cold, and the president of the United States had been assassinated. Audrey desperately tried to salvage what she could, but the remainder of the shooting was a struggle.

As usual, she was exhausted at the end of the filming and wanted to rest. Mel, however, was traveling throughout Europe trying to muster up funding for any kind of project for himself. While his wife's career was getting bigger and bigger, he was looking for roles, any roles. The closest he came to any project was in Spain, where he wanted to do a biographical movie on Queen Isabella. Unfortunately, the endeavor went bankrupt. In the end, he did a movie about the famed artist El Greco. Audrey felt it was her wifely duty to remain at his side during this trip.

In August of 1964, Audrey was shocked to learn that her father, Joseph Ruston, was still alive and living in Dublin. She hadn't heard from him in 25 years since he'd disappeared following the exposure of his fascist leanings. She and Ferrer headed to Ireland.

The reunion was a bit tense for everyone, including the stepmother Audrey had not known about. Joseph had married a woman thirty years younger than himself. He had kept up with his daughter's career but remained matter of fact about her fame. Too much time had passed for them to reestablish any type of familial relationship. Years later, Audrey mentioned that the reason Joseph had never gotten in touch with her was to save her the embarrassment of being known as the daughter of a fascist.

Mel and Audrey returned to the United States to attend the premiere of *My Fair Lady* in ten different cities. The more she saw the movie, the more Audrey regretted not doing her own singing. Hollywood gossip hag Hedda Hopper wrote, "With Marni Nixon doing the singing, Audrey Hepburn gives only half a performance." The reproach was difficult for Audrey to accept.

Still, the movie itself received extraordinary praise, as did Audrey's performance (not counting Hedda Hopper's little snipe). It received 12 Oscar nominations, but Audrey did not receive a nomination for Best Actress.

In an ironic twist, Julie Andrew, whom Warner had rejected for his movie for not being famous enough, was nominated for her role in *Mary Poppins.* The newspapers had fun with the situation, with the *Los Angeles Times* headlining, "Julie Andrews Chosen; Audrey Hepburn Omitted."

The drama extended to Oscar night. As a nominee, Julie would, of course, be there. By custom, the previous year's Best Actress, Patricia Neal, would be presenting the Best Actress award. But Patricia Neal had suffered from a series of strokes and was unable to attend. Audrey graciously offered to take her place.

With Julie and Audrey sitting only a row apart, every camera was ready, if not to say anxious, for some good old-fashioned rivalry and cat-fighting between the two. How disappointing that the two gracious British ladies embraced, posed happily for pictures, with Julie muttering, "I can't believe I won."

Chapter Nine

Divorce

"I was born with an enormous need for affection, and a terrible need to give it."

—Audrey Hepburn

Audrey's next film, *How to Steal a Million*, was another comedy, like *Charade.* Audrey plays the daughter of a scoundrel, Charles Bonnet, who enjoys forging famous artworks. This becomes a problem when a famous sculpture he has replicated accidentally ends up in a museum. He knows he won't be able to fool the museum experts after they do an authenticity test and his reputation will be ruined. To solve the problem, his daughter, Nicole, played by Audrey, plans to steal the statue from the museum before anyone becomes the wiser.

For this theft, she hires a burglar named Simon Dermott, who is played by Peter O'Toole. Nicole knows Dermott because he attempted to rob her and her father of a Van Gogh. Obviously, she couldn't report him because it would have exposed her father's forgeries. But now, she needs his talents to steal in order to save her father. Dermott agrees to do so.

Nicole has no idea that the burglar is actual an investigator who plans to put her and her father behind bars.

The following day, they go to the museum to examine the security. When Dermott attempts to steal the statue, he sets off the alarm. Quickly surrounded by police and museum guards, he manages to convince them that the alarm must have gone off by mistake. When Dermott and Nicole are alone again, he tells her he knows the statue is a fake. He is more successful during a second robbery attempt and manages to get the statue.

Dermott confronts Nicole and admits that he is an art historian specializing in theft. He'll take the statue safely out of the country to protect her father. Since they both realize they are attracted to each other, they go to Paris to elope, and her father promises to give up his forgeries.

Mel remained in Switzerland while Audrey filmed in Paris. After almost a dozen years of marriage, they seemed to have lost the initial passion. Rumors, whether true or false, of an affair between Audrey and O'Toole didn't help matters. When she returned to Switzerland, they settled down to find a real home. They found the perfect farmhouse in Tolochenaz, an hour outside of Geneva. Settling into their new home had a beneficial effect on their relationship. Audrey soon found herself pregnant again. Unfortunately, it ended in another miscarriage.

In 1967, Mel and Audrey left Sean in the care of a babysitter and traveled to Los Angeles to do *Wait Until Dark* for Jack Warner. Audrey was to play a young blind woman pursued by three thugs. Mel was hired as a producer. He drove Warner crazy with his expenditures, which included the building of an English tea garden where Audrey and the rest of the cast could enjoy refreshments.

The constant power struggle was difficult for Audrey. She realized by now that the marriage was floundering. They were only together for the sake of their son. Another problem was that Audrey wanted to cut down on the time she spent on her career and enjoy more time with Sean. That didn't go over well with Mel, who mostly only worked on projects on which Audrey worked. If she didn't work, neither did he.

By September of that year, the Ferrers announced that they were separating, but no mention was made of a divorce. By the following year, however, divorce proceedings were underway in Switzerland. Audrey had been the main breadwinner throughout most of their marriage. The Swiss legal details were kept confidential, but their friends were under the impression that Mel made out quite well for himself. At least Audrey received full custody of Sean, as was the norm in those days. Mel had visitation rights but could not take the boy outside of Switzerland.

Audrey was approaching 40, a difficult age in which to find herself alone. She had no idea what the future would hold for her. Fortunately, happiness was closer than she expected.

Chapter Ten

Late Life and Work for UNICEF

"I went into rebel country and saw mothers and their children who had walked for ten days, even three weeks, looking for food, settling onto the desert floor into makeshift camps where they may die. . . . The 'Third World' is a term I don't like very much, because we're all one world. I want people to know that the largest part of humanity is suffering."

—Audrey Hepburn

While her divorce was being finalized in 1968, Audrey was persuaded to join a cruise on the Aegean Sea on French tycoon Paul-Louis Weiller's yacht. It was just the diversion she needed. She left Sean in the care of her mother.

Also on the cruise was an attractive Italian doctor named Andrea Mario Dotti. Dotti was an amusing playboy and nine years younger than Audrey, but that didn't stop Audrey from pursuing a shipboard romance. Following the cruise, they kept in touch. She visited him in Rome, and he came to Tolochenaz. His mother was a Contessa, and the family quite wealthy, so there was no risk Dotti was romancing her for her money.

Audrey had many questions to consider. Could she move to Rome, where he lived? Could a movie star such as herself adjust to the life of a member of a non-acting patrician family? Whatever her reservations may have been, Audrey managed to charm Dotti's entire family. By Christmas, he presented her with an engagement ring. Knowing that the paparazzi would haunt them, they were married quickly in January of 1969. Her wedding dress was, of course, designed by Givenchy.

Following a quick honeymoon, the couple moved into a large apartment in Rome. This was Audrey's first real experience of being a housewife. Dotti left for work each day while Audrey puttered around the house, went out to lunch, and did some shopping. She turned 40 a few months later and found herself pregnant. Considering her history of miscarriages, she was extremely nervous. As a precaution, she spent most of her pregnancy in bed.

Regrettably, Dotti turned into somewhat of a casanova. While his wife was at home, he was seen in the latest fashionable nightclubs with an array of lovely ladies. Ever happy to highlight a scandal, the papers reported that one of his lady friends was young enough to be Audrey's daughter.

Meanwhile, Audrey gave birth to a son, Luca, on February 8, 1970. She withdrew from making movies until 1975, when she filmed *Robin and Marian*, the story of Robin Hood and Lady Marian in middle age. She hadn't acted for almost a decade and was now 46 years old. While she was away filming, Dotti was enjoying a happy nightlife without his wife. Divorce seemed like the only solution, and the couple officially split in 1982.

At the time of the divorce, Audrey had already been dating actress Merle Oberon's widower, Robert Wolders, for two years. They would stay together for the rest of Audrey's life, and she claimed that Robert was her one true love.

Most of Audrey's time was now spent working as an ambassador for UNICEF. She visited Africa and saw some of the devastating results of the famine that was starving and killing children. She gave a multitude of interviews to raise the public's awareness of this tragic situation. For several years, she tirelessly visited countries in an attempt to improve their situation in regards to food, clean water, immunization, and education. For her efforts, she received the Presidential Medal of Freedom in 1992. Audrey Hepburn, the actress, had morphed into Audrey Hepburn, the humanitarian.

Audrey eventually died of a rare form of abdominal cancer on January 20, 1993. She passed away peacefully during the night at age 63. Many dignitaries attended her funeral in her beloved Tolochenaz in Switzerland. Both of her exes were there. Elizabeth Taylor, Givenchy, Gregory Peck, and representatives from the Dutch royal family were all present to say goodbye to one of the most iconic actresses of all time.

Conclusion

It is difficult to think of Audrey Hepburn without imagining a charmed life. Born into a life of luxury, Audrey was the flawless daughter of Dutch nobility. When she turned to acting, she was an immediate success, winning critical raves with her first movie and those thereafter. Her beauty and regal grace simply couldn't be ignored. Givenchy designed most of her movie wardrobe, and as a result, Audrey Hepburn became as famous for her designer gowns as she was for her looks and charm.

Remarkably, most people don't know the real backstory behind this

Givenchy girl, one which was forged in the fires of World War II when Audrey spent the better part of the war in the grasp of the Nazi occupiers. Starvation, deprivation, and fear were daily occurrences during those five long years. After her uncle was cruelly executed by the Nazis, Audrey's whole family became part of the Dutch resistance movement.

Her experiences during the war and her later work and travel in the poverty-stricken regions of Africa were a million miles away from her life as a Hollywood fashionista. Perhaps these irreconcilable aspects of Audrey Hepburn's persona were what made her so intriguing to watch on the silver screen, turning her into one of the greatest legends of the Golden Age of Hollywood.

Bibliography

Ferrer, Sean (2005). Audrey Hepburn, an Elegant Spirit.

Gitlin, Martin (2009). Audrey Hepburn: A Biography.

Harris, Warren G. (1994). *Audrey Hepburn: A Biography.*

Heatley, Michael (2012). Audrey Hepburn: In Words and Pictures.

Matzen, Robert (2019). Dutch Girl: Audrey Hepburn and World War II.

Spoto, Donald (2006). Enchantment: The Life of Audrey Hepburn.

Vermilye, Jerry (1995). The Complete Films of Audrey Hepburn.